MIXED NUTS AND CHARACTER CAKE

MIXED NUTS AND CHARACTER CAKE

Boot

Library of Congress Control Number: 2011911986
ISBN: Hardcover   978-1-4653-3554-8
                 Softcover   978-1-4653-3553-1
                 Ebook   978-1-4653-3555-5

This book was printed in the United States of America.

To order additional copies of this book, contact:
Xlibris Corporation
1-888-795-4274
www.Xlibris.com
Orders@Xlibris.com
101849

DEDICATION

I would like to dedicate this book to my sister Patricia Armstrong who always believed in me and my ability to accomplished great things in life. Thanks Pat for always being there for me and encouraging me to dream and to act on those dreams.

I also like to thank my daughter Bianca who has always been an inspiration for all I've done and continuing to do. You are a truly beautiful spirit and as much a friend as a daughter. Mommy loves you dearly.

To my son Christopher, you've made your mom very very proud of you. You are the Rock of our family and so dear to my heart. You are a great husband and father to six of my grandchildren, Brittney, Jamon, De Andrea, Alexis, Shantella, and our beloved and departed Christopher, Jr.

Much love to my daughter-in-law, Charisse Hankinson Cephus, you are special to me, and to my grandbaby Kamaria Cephus and great grand Sah'nnrya.

Thanks to my ex-husband Ricard Rivera for waiting on me hand and feet as I typed out my manuscript. You've been a great friend these 23 years we've known each other. It's too bad we turned out to be better friends than lovers-smile.

CHAPTER 1

IT WAS AUGUST and extremely hot, like those dog days of August usually are in the middle of the month. As in the past few months, I could barely bring myself to get out of bed. This dam depression was pressing my mind like it would explode if I did not shut it down. I was so low in psychic, emotion, and spirit. This is the nature of the disease of depression, bipolar, and post-traumatic stress disorder, all of which I have been diagnose.

"Low in psychic" is major depression, recurrent, and severe for me. I am also bipolar II. A term used to refer to people who experience both lows and highs emotionally and psychologically. They have a manic phase that is experienced as well, not just as often as the depression. Then there is bipolar I where the individuals' primary symptom is extreme mania. Even with all the information and commercializing about mental illness, the media still gets excessively excited when it learns of artists, celebrities, and other famous persons that are diagnosed with bipolar disease. There is a fine line between sanity and insanity. I'll give you some statistics that will amaze you, especially those among the gifted, talented, and famous.

I was recently watching the Oprah Winfrey's Show and learned that Catherine Zeta Jones, an award winning actress and the wife of actor Michael Douglas, suffers bipolar. It is acknowledged by science that bipolar and other mental illness is a common condition that can be debilitating. For each person with depression and/ or bipolar disease, the experience can be very different.

There are so many famous people with the disease as stated earlier, that it will put us in "awe." Just to name a famous celebrity, Sally Fields, very artistic and talented was one of the first to speak out about her bipolar illness. But there are a whole host of new, younger, rich, and famous who other think is just ambitious, but really they are manic-depressive with all the signs and symptoms of bipolar. Charlie Sheen is in denial about his bipolar but eventually his behavior will land him where he is forced to get help, or he'll end up like Michael Jackson, whom I believe was also bipolar.

Another example of just how bipolar disorder is viewed by most people; remember Colonel Powell, former Secretary of Defense under President George Bush. He did not choose to run for president because of his wife's' bipolar. He did not want her to experience the media attention that was sure to follow should he had chosen to run for the office of presidency.

It is not uncommon for those individuals who have suffered any type of physical, emotional, and/or sexual abuse to end up being bipolar. In fact, as a professional scientist and someone who experienced emotional and sexual abuse, all that genius produced by us as artists in some form or another, is due to having such illness. Yet, bipolar left untreated can also cause many problems and some will end up in the criminal justice system like Lindsey Lohan.

Professionals in the field of psychiatry say that a disease of mental illness is not unlike diabetes, cancer, or heart problems. Instead of being a physical component of the body that is ailing, it is the mind that is ill. It is known to affect eighty-five percent of our geniuses and artists, actors, actresses, and even a few politicians. Abraham Lincoln was known to be bipolar. Still, there is such negativity and degradation associated with mental illness, in particularly bipolar. Even In the twenty-first century this disease is not something people are comfortable talking about.

Mental illness has such a stigma that this is one of several reasons I'm having this break down at this time. Being a therapist/counselor put me in a position where I could not be honest with colleagues and/or superiors without fear of some form of reprisal. I got tired of being schizophrenia. This term is simply used to describe how inconsistent my behavior would be at times. I had days of grandiosity, thinking I was invincible and could do anything. Although these were times I got a lot of work done, I usually also told coworkers "off" and just what I thought of them. They called me "Ms. Blunt", saying I was high-strung and highly confident in my job. After all, I had worked in the prison business for almost thirty years.

More to the point, mostly everyone I worked with in the prison system had "little to none "clinical skills for evaluating mental illness. They mostly "chalked" it up to having a stressful day because of the prison environment we worked in, or a stressful week or two, in my case. Had I had a fairly knowledgeable supervisor they would have realized I was truly bipolar, and not just malingering (faking crazy), as some people tend to do for some kind of personal gain. When I was not in a manic phase I would isolate myself and be distanced, quiet, and depressed. My energy level would be low and my work pace slowed considerable, but no one paid me much attention unless I was manic and trying to be the star of the week, or sometimes of the month, in my case.

My basic personality is of someone who is a progressive thinker, outwardly friendly and sociable. Most people in and outside of my department liked and respected me for my knowledge of corrections and my professionalism. I had worked in all departments except as an officer and in the medical unit. I worked the mental health unit for one year, general population for two years, and the diagnostic unit for the last fifteen years, and this was all at Metro State Prison, maximum security for female offenders with one death row inmate.

CHAPTER 2

THOSE PERSONS WITH the latter of the mental illnesses mentioned post trauma stress disorder, are not clearly distinguished from bipolar simply because the two tend to go together. I will talk more about mental illness but for now I want to introduce you to my "mixed nuts and character cake" women. I'm going to start by telling how that August day in 2010, started out for me and landed me in a small five-by-four cell with only the floor for me to sit or lay down on. I knew before that day was over I had to take some kind of action to shock myself into another mode of being. I tried getting through the day during my usual pacing up and down, slapping myself in the face and longing for the courage to drive onto that train track. It is like a ritual that I go through before I finally make the choice to check myself into the hospital for my bipolar episodes. This being episode nine or ten, since age fourteen. Dam, at fifty-four one would think this shit wouldn't still be happening to me of all people. Hell, I have a Master Degree in Clinical Psychology. I spent all those years working in a psychiatric hospital and later jails and prisons. I got to work with some of the most difficult populations in our universe, and not to "toot my own horn, "I was dam good at it. This is in spite that for many years I have had a disease that there are those who see such illness as abhorrent and the individual as being continuously crazy.

In the past two years I have been diagnosed with two types of physical problems that compound my mental illness and have affected my ability to function in a professional capacity any longer. In 2008, I was diagnosed with degenerative disc disease, and in 2010, atrial fibrillation. This is why I find myself at the cross-road of life and once again in crisis. I had plan to work until age seventy-five, or until I could not do the job. I had been praying and hoping for a long healthy life like my great-granny Lonnie, who lived actively until age ninety-five and died at one hundred and three.

It is my great-grandma Lonnie I have to think for my obsession with trains and killing myself by sitting my car right on the tracks when it is known a train will be coming. My cousin Vicki and I would be awakened by my Aunt Corinne and Grandma Lonnie who use the time the train ran every morning to awaken us for school. There was a train that ran every morning around 5:30 am, and at 5:00 pm in the evening. The evening train was used to make sure we got our homework done and start getting prepared for school the next day; eating super and ironing cloths if they had not already been done. Needless to say sometimes the train was off schedule and really caused big problems. One morning Grandma Lonnie had us up out of bed, fed cereal and bananas, and dressed for school. When the kitchen stove clock was checked, and only because the day break we were waiting for never happened, it turned out to be only 3:45 am. We all lay back down fully dressed for school.

I, along with my cousin Vicki was raised up by two elderly women, a mother and daughter, Corrine and Lonnie. The train tracks ran about a half mile behind the little white two-bed room house my granny owned. Corrine did not have children and she sort of adopted me and my blood uncle Caul. Caul was ten years older and I was only nine months when my biological mother and father who is Cauls' biological brother, allowed Corrine to keep me over nights with her. She had her own house that we had lived in, she, Uncle Doc, Caul, and me, until uncle Doctor died and she and I moved in with great-Grandma Lonnie.

By then Caul had gone onto be a part of the "sit-ins" during Martin Luther King, Jr.'s area. Then he was drafted into the Vietnam War in 1968. I had a grudge against my mom thinking she gave me away because she did not love me. It would be many years later after becoming an adult that I could look back and see that she allowed Corrine to raise me out of love. Mom was twenty-three years old with five children to rise with a husband who had left the air force and refused to work hard to provide for their children.

Mom worked two and three jobs to be able to care for her children including me. And Corrine dotted on me and provided me with a good education and nice clothes to wear to school. Lonnie was Vicki's grandmother and my great grandmother. She was probably close to seventy-five and Aunt Corrine sixty. Great-Grandma Lonnie had been a young mother at fifteen. This was not young for back in the day when women married early. And definitely not so young when you consider that my cousin Vicki and I both got pregnant at ages twelve years old.

Because of this Vicki was sent to live with an alcoholic and physically abusive father in Battle Creek Michigan, and I was sent two houses down from my great-granny to live with my mother and father. By that time I was damaged goods. The rape and molestation by my uncle Caul had turned me into a very promiscuous girl who always wanted sex because I had been trained up in it from the cradle, so to speak. So when my cousin's cousin-in-law came to visit one day as I clean their home, and the eighteen year old football player asked me to let him teach me to French kiss, I said yes. That first and only time I lost my virginity I was pregnant. I was eight months pregnant before anyone found out about me. I wore girdles, two and three, to hide my pregnancy, and I put tomato ketchup in the bed to fool my old aunt and grandma that I was still having a menstruate cycle.

Sex has been for me for most of my life the only way I felt love. Love and sex was one in the same, and when I got any kind of rejection from a boy, and later men, it devastated my ego. Now at fifty and since my last fling with a 24 year old at forty-two, I have learned there are such things as lust, sex, and love, and plutonic love, and there is such a monumental difference between the four kinds of feelings. It saddens me sometimes that all my life lessons came in my early fifties. But I have learned to love me, and this has been no easy task by any means!

Being promiscuous and confusing feelings and emotions is not a problem at this stage. I think this is why my last stay at the "nut" farm was truly my last" redo". I can say this because I have had a healing experience. My psychiatric, Dr. Valerie Honblue" has that healing touch. In all my life she is the first to genuinely give me a psych homework that got to the core of my being. Some of us have those same type gifts. Ophra have touched thousands, we just touch a few lives. But saving one life is a miracle and to be commended for sure. I have always prayed for the strength to help just one person move beyond suffering, and if I just happen to help three or four, well Lord my destiny has been fulfilled and I can be humbled and thankful.

CHAPTER 3

I LOVED MY job in spite of my many complaints about the state system. Working with other people with problems that I could relate to was catharsis for me. I also tried to bring a humanistic-clinical approach to my counseling style. I genuinely cared about the inmates/clients' that I was responsible for as a Behavioral Specialist/Counselor. The inmates would often express a desire for me to be their counselor when they complimented me; telling me that they liked that I seemed sincere and was down-to-earth with them. This just means I treated them as a human being without judgment for their past histories and/or crimes. I focused on how they could be productive persons now and once they left prison. The judge sentences the offender and that is their punishment. Prison is to protect the public until their sentence ends, and to protect them from self-harm or harm of another. Therefore, I leave the murders and baby killers to be judged by the Almighty. I treated all inmates the same regardless of their crime.

My intention here is not to get all serious about my personal or professional life. I am writing to tell you about my stay in the "nut" hospital. It is a story that is sad but in some instances hilarious. This will depend on your sense of humor. Jack Nicholson's "One Who Flew over the Cuckoo Nest" will look like men on Rebecca's' Sunny-Brook Farm compared to "Mixed Nuts and Character Cake". This is what it was like everyday living with forty something women "caged" together and unable to go anywhere alone except to the day room if no activity is scheduled for that hour. Then there were usually several others spread out, or in a corner trying to find themselves some alone Time.

The hospital was designed to look like a college campus dormitory. Each unit or floor has approximately forty-two rooms that start out from a huge circular room that we called the day room or activity/group room. There is a nursing station area, a pantry room with micro wave and refrigerator with juices and milk and crackers and cereal for snacking on after the cafeteria closed at 7:00 pm. There was also a laundry room. The laundry room was well used because most t of us shows up at the hospital with nothing more than the cloths on our backs. Unless you got family members to bring you cloths and toiletries you may find some donated in your size if the hospital has any on hand. The rooms ran off the circular part into halls that had two to a room. You did not get to pick your roommate. It was just like any other normal hospital room. I had two different roommates during my stay. Because each day someone left and someone new would take their place. It was a revolving door just like any prison.

Everything was locked up and only if you had progressed could you have a razor for shaving and then only in the present of a nurse. The only exit was the door leading to our private dining area where we lined up by name and was escorted to breakfast, lunch, and dinner. The food was superb and there was a variety to choose from. After breakfast we got our second smoke break. If you got up really early the med nurse would be nice enough to let you have one after vital signs and medication. I and a whole lot of others usually did not miss a smoke break. There is some strange kind of relationship between mental illness and cigarette smoking. I believe the smoke blocks certain thoughts and help calm the nerves. This sounds to be a logical explanation any way.

The women all sit in clustered groups of five or six when on free time and would spend it in the smoke area. Our days were structured with each hour or two being a scheduled block activity or group meeting where we learned basic coping skills, triggers that lead to our illness, and how to keep from having a relapse. Mainly stopping medications was the number one problem causing relapse. And people like me who was having financial problems to the point that medications were not being bought on time, in many instances. I had to skip a week just to pay a light bill sometimes. My money was not adding up with the way the economy was changing, but I am hanging in like everyone else around me and waiting for shit to get better.

Sometimes we can't always get to a safe haven like Orchard Landing so until we can some of us will call up the mental health hotline/blog. This is what we usually get when my girls and I call up:

When Cherie dials up the hotline she gets this message: "If you have a nervous disorder, please fidget with the pound button until a representative comes on line."

If you happen to have bipolar disorder like Sue, Helen, Wendy and Kellie, you get "please leave a message after the beep. Or before the beep. Or after the beep. Please wait for the beep.

Tina and Bonnie, "If you got post trauma stress disorder, slowly hang up the phone and dial 911."

Janet, "If you have obsessive compulsive disorder, please press 1 repeatedly."

Ms. Margret, "If you have low self-esteem, please hang up. All our representatives' are busy."

Wendy and Helen, "if you are suffering from paranoid schizophrenia, we know who you are and what you want. Stay on the line so we can trace your call."

When Sue called up the manic depressive line she was told, "It doesn't matter which button you push no one will answer."

Helen, "if you are delusional, press seven and your call will be transferred to the mother ship."

Out of the eight of us Helen was the sweetest person you could ever meet, though she had some serious problems in that most medications had an adverse effect on her. Nothing was working for her so she signed on for "electrical shock therapy."(EST). Helen was soft spoken, rather quiet, and stayed pretty much to her. But then if she was up and about she would join in on conversations and always encouraged us to love ourselves because she loved all of us. Those who came in with no money or had no real family support Helen would buy them cigarettes, give them money for the vending machines, and care for them as if they were her children.

She was probably forty-five with two boys and a girl that she dotted on just like us patients. But she was seriously depressed with a schizoid personality disorder. She would be lucid one moment and then flip very quickly into a catatonia state of being. This is where the person loses contact with reality. Often times Helen could be found sitting alone in the big lobby while most of the other patients were in their rooms. She would be crying, the tears rolling down her face and she would be rigged holding tight to a tissue paper. She had big pretty eyes, a round baby face and she was petite and around one hundred fifty pounds and maybe she was five feet two inches. She had pretty long black hair worn straight with a bang and parted to the side. She was a beautiful black girl but with a serious illness.

CHAPTER 4

THESE WERE EIGHT women with all these different diagnosis's going on and we meet on a nut ward and developed sudo-friendships while stabilizing on psychotropic medications. Some people may find the word "nut" offensive, insulting, or derogatory. As in my title "Mixed Nuts And Character Cake, this is intended to humor you, as most mentally ill person's behavior does. Paradoxically, the other part of the title" Character Cake is to let you see the sweet nature of many of the characters in this story. The reader will get some insight of what goes on in a psychiatric hospital. Many of which are designed like country clubs or resorts where you go to heal the mind and body. Orchard Landing Behavioral Health Unit was no Betty Ford, but it was plush with beautiful sceneries of trees, flowers, tennis court, and swimming pool. And like at Betty Ford or any other psychiatric hospital there was structure and a 24 hour schedule to be followed. In this sense the" nut" unit is just like a prison camp. The doctors are the wardens. Their advice and instructions must be followed above everything else that goes on.

Life can take many turns along that journey we all must travel. Who knew I would spiral into depression again. It had been ten years since my last "rodeo" at the" nut" ward. I have had eight or nine since age fourteen. At fifty-four I tend to get a memory lapse every now and then. This is the nature of the beast of age and mental illness. You tend not to be aware that your logic is slowly going and irrationality is taking completely over. The ritual

I talked about earlier is the first sign that it's time to go somewhere I can protect myself from myself. I had become majorly depressed, bipolar II, and post traumatically stressed out. In short order, I had become hopeless which equals suicidal thinking.

It is August 9, 2010, a sultry late afternoon, a clear blue sky with a faint smell of mowed grass and honey suckles waffling threw the air. Here I am crying rivers of tears and driving toward the train tracks that set a half mile from my job. I left work earlier under the pretext that my wrists and arms were aching from all the data input I had done that morning. This was a partial truth, except that when at work I spent so much of my energy and time hiding my illness that I was more emotionally and psychologically drained than from any physical exertion.

It was around 9:30 pm, by the time I drove myself from the rail road tracks I had been stalking that afternoon to Dekalb Medical Center. I was too fatigued to drive anywhere further. I'd never been to the psychiatric ward or knew how they would handle me as a potential suicide patient. I found out real quick when I found myself in 5 feet by 6 feet room. Nothing was in the room except me stripped of all my personal belongings. I had to stay there until I could be evaluated by a psychiatrist. I had never experienced anything like this before. I cried out to be released.

I tried bargaining telling them that I no longer wanted to kill myself. Finally after I screamed, yelled, and cursed, a guard and a nurse came in to give me some meds. I vaguely remember my conversation with the attending physician, but they decided to keep me on a "ten-thirteen" basis. This is a court order allowing the hospital to keep me for protection against doing bodily harm to myself, and because I had given them the plan on how I would carry out my suicide. The next morning I was transferred to Orchard Landing Behavioral Health Unit.

My two week stay at this "plush" psychiatric hospital in Atlanta, Georgia reminded me of a can of Planters Mixed Nuts where you have peanuts, pecans, cashews, almonds, brazil, hazel nuts, and few unknown nuts all mixed in together. I saw all of us mentally ill individuals as characters living, loving, and sharing together. It was an amazing experience and I think others who have been there will understand.

Those who have not will not only get some understanding of what it is to be a patient in a mental hospital, but will learn that maybe all those ups and down feelings they have been having may be one of the various diagnosis's like major depression, schizophrenia, bipolar, or post trauma stress disorder. Or, that all that drinking and drugging they are doing is because of one of the mentioned mental illness. It is not surprising that many mentally ill persons have a dual diagnosis of mental illness and substance abuse. Mental illness can be so painful that alcohol and drugs are used as analgesia. It is a negative way of coping with life stressors and it only compounds our problems. Yet, it is a way to cope and to survive the pain.

First, how do you deal with unbearable" gut "wrenching" pain? You feel like an alien, a non-being who is here on this planet of infinity of beings. Except you feel alone and there is a disassociation with everything and everybody. The first to go is the psychic part of your mind. You become irrational and illogical. Your cognition and your thinking are disorganized. What you do or say does not make sense to others. You try to control this type of thinking but are unable to do so. It is at this point that I become disconnected to my God, Buddha, or whomever we chose to call our higher power. Once the psychic and spirit part of our being has left your emotions becomes volatile and unpredictable. Suicide or getting rid of the psychic pain is a constant, repetitive thought, and depending on the "depth of the pain and suffering it is preferable to the continued "toss-salad" thinking and desperation of helplessness and hopelessness. Then you start to think of the way you should murder yourself.

Scientific data suggest that women prefer less degrading means of dying like taking pills, cutting their wrist, or driving their car onto a train track. This is something that is quick but does not make them ugly in death. Men on the other hand, usually do a gunshot to the head, driving off a bridge, or sitting up a situation where the cops will have to take them out. Once thinking has progressed to this point one must seek out protection for themselves. It is time to go to the "rodeo", as my friend Sue would put it. This means going to a place where there are people going through the same feelings and thoughts as you and there are doctors and nurses to take care of you and get you back to planet earth.

The women I met were wild, witty, and very "raw" in their behavior. Of course now we are talking about women who have the commonality of all being unstable mentally. Let me interject here for those who don't know the difference, Personality is concrete, it is who you really are and it comes through even in the midst of craziness. I met many women with beautiful spirits. Like Sue, who was always appearing very normal and then there were other moments when she sit with her legs cross and she would rock back and forth in one of her incoherent-crazy mentally ill episodes.

Sue and the others did not hesitate to tell their life stories, or as Sue would constantly refer to her stays in the hospital, "this isn't my first rodeo, and I'm sure with going through this divorce it won't be my last." Sue is forty-two; five-six, red headed, and was always well dress with matching red finger-nail and toe polish. She was a beauty in spite of admitting to shedding two hundred pounds with stomach surgery. She was classy, bright and witty. We hit it off from the very beginning, not that it helped that we both smoked Bs&Hs(Benson & Hedges cigarettes) that are referred to as "bitches and hoes".

CHAPTER 5

THERE WAS NO subject off limits for us from music, politics, race relations, to how it was for the two of us growing up in the state of Alabama in the 60's and 70's during the era of segregation. Sue was white with Indiana and Irish blood. And I lived with a "white", ex-husband, and an interracial daughter. Both of us were intellectual types and liked to discuss people, places, and situations in depth. We are also passionate individuals with a true love for man and humanity in spite of us both being bipolar.

The two of us really "clicked". The others had just as much heart. I had a special relationship with my roommate, Cherie who was "white", intellectual, and formerly a social worker for adults with mental retardation in a community-living setting. Cherei and I spend many sleepless nights and days talking about writing about our experiences with all the others. I have yet to hear from her, or any the others in our pack. We all promised to keep in touch, but for reasons that are not very well understood we chose not to do so. I will re-visit this subject at some other place in my story just to give my own personal reason for not reaching out to those I met during my two week stay at Orchard Landing Behavioral Health Center.

Cherie had been molested by her brother who was a few years older than she was and she was bipolar 1, meaning she had more episodes of manic than depression. She and her brother were estranged and rarely had contact. However her mother had recently passed away and the brother had been trying to have her declared mentally ill and incompetent to handle her part of the estate that she was to inherit. Chereri had been homeless from time to time and had been hospitalized on several occasions and this is what was being used against her. She had gotten off her meds and like the rest of us was there to stabilize on meds. She was obsessing and believed her brother wanted to poison her. The only other relative was an uncle who Cherei claims was siding with her brother.

Cherei was talkative and hypered and spent many hour repeating over and over how her brother had mistreated her all her life and that no one in the family believed that he had molested her. I could relate to Cherie's' constant obsession and talking about her past trauma. After all, when no one believes you it is just that much more devastating. All of us women were survivors of sexual, physical, and emotional abuse. We had not yet "healed". There is a vast difference in being a survivor and being" healed". This is one reason that we all ended up at the "rodeo" again. Sue, Cherie, Helen, Janet, Ms. Margaret, Wendy, Kellie, and me. The eight of us were hilarious in spite of being emotionally and psychologically ill. We did a lot of crying and a lot of laughing during our stay at the Orchard Landing Hospital.

Cherie and I would laugh ourselves to sleep at nights over something funny or weird that had happen during our group time together, or when we were on one of our cigarettes breaks. We all had to be out of bed by six-thirty a.m. for medication and vital sign regiments. Breakfast was at seven-thirty and you were not allowed to sleep in unless you were on room restriction due to some health problem, or your thorozine had you incapacitated.

This reminds me of that first night spend at Dekalb in that jail cell. I have never been in jail and it freaked me out. I got more understanding and empathy of how being locked in a cell must feel like for prisoners. I'm in a hospital cell but it sure as hell felt like incarceration. I knew the only way out was to get through to the psychiatrist who in this sense is the warden. The nurses are the deputy wardens, and the mental health assistances are the correction officers or jailers. They can't do anything without doctors' orders. I understood the need for the rules and regulations and the structure. It is to protect the patient from harm of self and others. Yet, like any other regular patient in the throes of their illness, I acted out verbally threatening and complaining of mistreatment. Like prisoners my free will had been taken, and in both cases there are good reasons.

I was knocked out on tranquilizers. All I remembered was awakening on my ride to Orchard Landing. I was being transferred there from DeKalb Psychiatric unit where I had spent the night. The ambulance attendants', a black male and white female, told me I had put in a request to be transferred and they had been told I had been verbally and physically combated about staying at their facility; mainly because they were none smoking and I had wanted to smoke. Orchard Landing was a smoking facility with such privilege given outside in special areas.

Patient's free will is restored slowly as we progress by getting the right medications and positive effects, along with going to scheduled groups, and following your individualized treatment plan. The prisoner also has a treatment plan to follow. How ironic that life as a mental health patient correlates so well with those given sentences in our state penal system. Patient and staff in both cases must work closely together. They all bring everything that they are to that relationship. Therefore, it is essential that staff have their own emotions and lives in control, or it will spill over into the relationship with patients and can cause patients to be worse off than before they came into treatment or prison as the case may be.

These are my sentiments considering that I have spent much of my life in both places. Only in the prison setting I was a Professional employer as mention earlier. Now I am a patient talking about my extraordinary experiences with women who became comrades, supporters, and very sweet and sharing of all of themselves. In being with women suffering from like illnesses as myself, I began to feel healed, not just a survivor as I had always labeled myself. Before my time spent at Orchard Landing treatment had been of minimum help. I was able to shelve my stuff, my feelings, and appear normal on a daily basis, until something unexpected would trigger symptoms of depression or mania. When I had manic phases at work I got a lot done. I could work circles around my colleagues. They liked me for this but I don't think they realized I was in a manic state. For the most part I had been a loner at work and mostly in my private life. But my personality is such that I am a very sociable person, friendly, and love helping others with their problems. That is why I work in serving people. I don't have time to think about my own ugly experiences of being molested between ages one and eleven years old. But remembering is what happens even when I am trying very hard not to.

I remember the molestation and the rape, but it has been years of therapy that has convinced me it probably started right after I moved into the home with my Uncle Caul and Aunt Corrine around age one. Caul was a very, very, handsome man even in his brutality of me as a child. I remember all the girls and women "swooned "over him. Even my mother loved her brother-in-law so much. She called him her black Rock Hudson. And of course most pedophiles are charming people pleasers. They are "seduction" and "conning" at its' best. They seem ordinary and nothing stands out except their easy going, friendly nature. Caul was a poster boy in school. He was an all-around sportsman and very good in football, basketball, and baseball. And he always had the pretties and most popular girls. He was approximately 6.5 ft., Carmel smooth unblemished skin, hairy chest, mustache and a hell of pair of bow-legs with an eight-pack stomach. He was good looking in capital letters. And he dressed to show off all that he had physical-wise. This is how I remembered my uncle Caul. This is what I wrote in my journal when I journeyed back in time from birth to age ten:

Lying in bed with uncle Caul, he tickles me as we play in bed. I giggle. He straddles me. He takes his thing and rubs it around my mouth and tells to me lick it like I do my lollipops. I lick because I really like candy. He rubs it on my neck, on my chest, and down to my stomach. It does not hurt. It smells funny. Then he gets me all wet and sticky. Then he rubs the wet stuff all over me. I taste it by accident. It tastes funny. It's on my mouth, my neck, my stomach, and where I pee-pee. Then he wipes me clean. He cuddles and snuggles close to me. We go to sleep. Tomorrow he will give me my favorite candy, a black cow and a sugar daddy. I smile. I dream.

Like many of the women I spent time with at Orchard Landing Behavioral Health Unit, childhood sexual abuse was a common theme among our lives. Then there are those who fail to comprehend how abuse is so difficult to get over and move on in life. Those are the people I tell this to. It's something an abused woman wrote.—"Why are you dragging this up now? Why? Because it has controlled every facet of my life. It has damaged me in every possible way. It has destroyed everything in my life that has been of value. It has prevented me from living a comfortable emotional life. It has prevented me from being able to love clearly. It took my children away from me. I haven't been able to succeed in the world. If I had a comfortable childhood, I could be anything today. I know that everything I don't deal with now is one more burden I have to carry for the rest of my life. I don't care if it happened 500 years ago. It has influence me for all that time, and it does matter. It matters very much____Jennierose Lavender, 47 year old survivor. (From the book" The Courage to Heal").

Like Jennierose, I, Tina, Cherie, Janet, and many of my other peers suffer from childhood sexual abuse that resulted in major depression, bipolar, and PTSD. Tina's childhood was filled with much horror. The physical abuse was horrendous. The things she shared in group and in our quiet times together was unimaginable and my mind barely comprehended how a father does such things to a child. Her father torched her before and after he made her do all kinds of perverted acts on him. He even hog tied her and beat her severely for all of her early childhood and adolescent years. The depth of her sadness can be seen in her deep beautiful blue eyes.

Tina was another character that was sweet as apple pie with a mixture of true southern girl, partly ignorant, and races toward blacks and Mexicans. In her bipolar moments she would us the nigger word loudly enough to offend someone and then finish with something about that's why Mexicans get the work now. Mostly, Tina cried and apologized for her inappropriate behavior. She would say "I am so sorry, over and over, and seemed sincere. I didn't get offended from my peers because I understood we were at the bottom trying desperately to hold on to sanity. Even though it would come and go at any moment until our medication restored us to full sanity. I knew all this from having come to the "redoes" many times before. Tina had been a number of times herself.

Tina had been born on a farm in South Georgia and had a very good work ethic. She was always cleaning up or moving about. Though restlessness is a symptom of bipolar. Tina was also brought up by a father who terrorized the family and took her out to their shed and sexually molested, raped and beat her from age seven to fourteen. At that age it was alleged that Tina nearly beat her sixty year old dad to death with a baseball bat. Her reputation also included beating two big as hell white male cops. She never served any prison time. It was a small town and everyone knew everyone else. Tina's ordeal "fucked her up royally", but she is a survivor like the rest of us. Every so often I think PTSD(Post Traumatic Stress Disorder) kicks us back into the past and it triggers our depression or bipolar, or whatever the illness may be that we suffer from.

This term was initially used to refer only to war veterans who had experienced combat and returned from the war with certain psychiatric symptoms. They had violent flashbacks and many used drugs and alcohol to cope. They were depressed and acted out in ways that affected their ability to live a normal life. Later the term was used to describe none veteran as well who had been exposed to some traumatic event over a time period. The trauma left a foot print that would always be there. It lays dominant until as I mentioned earlier a stressor cause it to flare up. On a final note, PTSD is nothing more than confusing the past with the present. Cherie can't seem to let her past go and neither can I.

This is also what makes mental illness such a difficult disease to treat. Our friend Janet was paralyzed from the waist-down and will never walk again. She has had many suicide attempts since living in a care-home that she does not like very well. She ended up in Orchard Landing after busting out of the care-home in her wheel chair and rolling down a steep hill into the middle of a four-way traffic intersection.

When I met Janet she was sitting in her electrical wheel chair reading the Atlanta Constitution. Every morning after breakfast and sometimes lunch this is what she did. It was apparent that she was an avid reader. She was smart and well spoken. The only problem is that I always ended up next to Janet at breakfast, lunch, and diner. She had a urine bag that was always nearly full and it smelled very bad. I would pretend it did not bother me because I did not want to offend a woman so vivacious even in her handy-cap. I admired her intellect and her spirit. She and I talked plenty of politics and sports. We both loved football. We talked about how we struggle to stay sane in an insane world. Janet was such a character and loveable person that everyone gravitated to her and when she told her story of driving her wheel chair down a steep hill into the middle of traffic it was hilarious the way she laugh and told about it. She says she is glad she was not hit or killed, because she never had given thought to how the person who might have killed her would be affected.

Janet had lived in a care home for the disabled for five years, Her mother had died of breast cancer and Janet did not want to be a burden to anyone else so she opted to live on her own. Her chief complaint was that the home did not help as often as was needed with her hygiene care. She didn't get a bath but twice a week, that is a full bath. This depressed Janet who had been a proud librarian. You could tell how she took pride in her dressing and grooming. She must have been approximately five feet seven, 140 pounds with straight, long black hair that hung freely down her back. She liked her shorts and sneakers and probably liked out-doors type of activities before her car accident that left her paralyzed from the waist down. Janet was a carrot cake to me. I love carrot cake too. Even if her urine bag was smelly most times, she was a sensitive and intelligent "nutty" character.

Janet was nutty in a funny kind of way, but Wendy was a certifiable "nut" and such a character that she missed her calling from Hollywood. She was a short woman, and not even five feet compared to all us women, but she had the loudest voice. She had that Neapolitan complex, "the little man" complex in female form. She not only talked loud, but she could out curse a sailor, and every other word was punctured with "mother-fucker" this, or that so and so "bitch". Usually these were reserved for the nursing staff that did not let her get her way. She liked messing with the men who ate lunch with us and participated in some groups Wendy was ghetto with a capital G and had spent most of her life in Baltimore, Maryland.

Wendy was forty-eight but seemed older. She had that hard-look from having drinked and drugged hard for most of her life. She always had something funny to say, or sometimes something embarrassing to say. I liked her, and her roommate Ms. Margaret liked her but not many of the other women. They thought she was racist because sometimes she would say things about "white people" that were offensive. Ms. Margaret was a fragile looking white woman age sixty-eight. Wendy was very protective of her and they seemed to have a really good relationship. Their relationship reminded me of a nanny taking care of her white superior mistress. But seeing how they were genuine friends showed me that like all seven of my other female comrades, in her heart she was not at all racist, and she too was sweet as a pineapple up-side-down cake which also describes her roommate Ms. Margaret.

Everyone used only their first name to maintain anonymity, but Margaret was the only one everybody addressed as Ms. It had to do with her being the oldest among the group and her character. She was very tall and slim. She had snow white shoulder length hair and was very graceful in her manners. She rarely smiles. Only Wendy could bring one out of her. She was chronically depressed and had been since her only child, a son, had committed suicide. According to Ms. Margaret her son had struggled with addiction to methamphetamines for many years. He got tired and took a shot-gun to his head and blew his brains out in front of his wife and their daughter. Ms. Margaret's husband said she had never recovered from this tragedy. Her husband was the step-father to her son. He spoke well of the boy saying he worked hard to care for his family but drugs got in the way and caused him to lose good jobs.

Because Ms. Margaret had a very supportive husband and it appeared they were fairly well off financially, some residents tried taking advantage of her. Wendy did not let this happen often. She would bluntly tell that person who was begging for money or cigarettes to get the hell on and leave Ms. Margaret alone. Wendy was street-wise and old-school in that she could easily pick up on those residents who were sociopaths and not just mentally ill. As I mentioned before some were there to appease the justice system and claiming drug addiction cause them to commit whatever the crime was that they were being charged or convicted on. This reminds me of our youngest and most popular group member, Kellie.

Kellie was twenty-eight years old, Italian, and mean as hell when something or someone "pissed" her off. At 6 feet tall and one hundred and seventy-five pounds, she could afford to be mean spirited. One Sunday morning I heard some commotion in the day room where everyone was lining up to get vital signs and medications. I walked into the room just as Kellie had walked up into the face of another resident and say "you fucking dog killer, I'll kill your ass "! She caught hold of the lady's neck with both hands around her throat and choked the poor woman to the floor. Then she let go of her and began punching her in the face with her fist.

The lady's nose was bleeding and her hair and clothes were in disarray. All of us women were yelling and screaming as two nurses kicked into action and pulled Kellie away. They admonished Kellie for attacking an old lady. It had been rumored that his one resident was there because she had poisoned her husband's dog with antifreeze. This incident was probably brought on by the fact that on that previous Saturday, we had pet therapy where volunteers bring in several dogs for us to pet and play with for an hour or two. Come to think of it the accused dog killer did not show up the day before for that particular activity, and nor did we see her all that previous afternoon. She was a smoker and did not even come out for smokes. Now I understood.

The lady obvious had not kept up with how Michael Vicks had been treated over his mistreatment of dogs. I even remember now other women chanting "kill the bitch." The incident was laughable only because the lady who was attacked did not get any serious injuries. On that same day Kellie was scheduled to be released. The incident should have been cause for her to stay on longer but she was released at her scheduled time.

Kellie was married with two boys ages ten and twelve. She was addicted to prescription pain medications, and was at the center for drug treatment. She was an emergency transportation attendant and seemed to like her job. Kellie was a real live character. I admired her "bluntness" and no-none sense attitude.

But it was obvious she had anger management problems to work on. She was not alone in this; I definite have had many problems in dealing with anger. More recently I've realized that I've been angry with my father for dying____so angry that it took two years for me to finally grieve and move on.

CONCLUSION

AT MY FATHER'S funeral I leaned over into the casket that held his body. I held him close to me for a long moment. I would truly miss him. He was more than my father, he was also my friend. They say funerals are for the living. This is too true. Because we don't just weep for the departed we weep also for ourselves. For the brevity of life. For its' ever accumulating insignificance. For the way we stumble through it, like foreigners without a map, making mistakes at every turn and curve in the road.

I gave a speech as the daughter of the deceased. I had been thinking of saying something about my father's life and what kind of father and friend he had been. I didn't know if I would be emotionally controlled enough so it was at the last minute before the silent reading of the obituary that I stood up and walked up to the microphone. My words were from the "heart" and the first were "my father was not a perfect man, but he was a good man." Later after the funeral my sister said to me that I had gotten a standing ovation—and that this was the first time at any funeral where this had happened that she had attended. I had only mention how my father always taught us to study the bible and live according to God's commandments. I also talked about how my family laughs a lot together and how both my mother and father liked to tell jokes and laugh together. They both should have been Hollywood comedies. They were so good at making everyone around them laugh from one of their jokes, or just coming out with something from the heart that was funny.

Since my father's death and in my grief I have come to realize that you never totally get over the pain of someone close to you dying. The pain is too big, too consequential. The person can only live with it, keep it buried deep down and go on with life. Being at a place like Orchard Landing where there was camaraderie, compassion, and constant support from peers and staff had a very powerful healing effect on my life in many different respects. One thing is that I gained a sense of peace with my father being where he was watching down over me just like when his spirit was here on earth.

I am sure that there were many others who had that same rewarding and healing of painful wounds as I did. There was constant positive feedback that we did as an activity first thing in the mornings and right before lights were out at nine-thirty each night. This helped to reintegrate and reinforce positive thinking and feeling. Peers are often times our biggest source of strength in the healing process. I believe that like prayer when there is more than one person seeking a source of energy that energy is returned two-fold so that the more people coming together for a common purpose the more that purpose will become a reality.

Out of all that was shared among us women, no one had time to be judgmental. We were too busy trying to work out our individual problems. Mind was whether or not I should take a disability leave from my job of seventeen years at the Women's Prison. Others had already been laid off and were in crisis over how to survive on a weekly unemployment check. Some had no home to return to and was looking for homeless shelters as a means of having a roof over their head. Many were skeptical about their future and this was very sad for me. I at least had a home and family support. Still I had begun to realize that my own regression and relapse had much to do with the fact that my uncle Caul was still very much a part of my family life. He was serving a life sentence for the murder of his second wife and three year old son, Bryant. He had another son fifteen at the time and he had stated during trial that he did not kill this son because he was afraid he would have wrestle with him because he was a big boy.

This cowardly statement by him made me sick to my stomach. Caul had also killed his first wife and two daughters Pam and Cassandra, ages seven and ten some twenty-three years earlier. He got off by reason of insanity after having served in the Vietnam War. He killed two wives and three children and my family still stands with him. What my mother never understood is that this man hurt me and he probably hurt his children sexually before he murdered them. "Sins of the Father" is what they called his story. The media perpetrated this man as a war hero who suffered post-traumatic stress disorder. After all, he had a purple heart and was an excellent Detroit Police Officer when all this happened, that is the first murders. He spent one year at Yislanta State Hospital, Michigan, and then was let go free to commit the same kind of murders again. The sad thing about this is that he is a pervert and a pedophile and no one has ever known about this.

When I told my mother when I was twenty-eight years old and having a bipolar episode, she said to me, "I don't believe that.

Why did you tell your father or me? Your dad would have killed him then and he would not have been around to kill all those people. I was stung! But I realized my mother did not ever like to face the truth of anything. She could not understand something if it did not happen to her. Then she went on to tell me of how this older man had tried to touch her when she was a girl and she hit his hand away and never had any more problem with him. She was in total denial of what had happened to me. She tells me now I should forgive him. Lord knows I've tried. But the damage to my life has been tremendous. I've never known a trusting, loving relationship with any man, and I believe it is because of my childhood trauma.

Yet, I am a survivor like my other ladies, Tina, Wendy, Sue, Janet, Helen, Kellie, and Ms. Margaret. It has been said that "character" is destiny! Perhaps, but timing plays one hell of a big role too! In the many years that I have worked with incarcerated women identified as bipolar or chronically depressed, and with those women I worked with in private and community agencies, ninety-nine percent of them had been either sexually, emotionally, psychologically, or physically abused, or some combination of several of these, or all of these. And for many of these survivors "going crazy" makes a lot of sense. When the pain gets too great we seek out ways to alleviate that pain. Some self-mutilate, attempt suicide, alcohol/drug addiction and isolation for others.

www.ingramcontent.com/pod-product-compliance
Lightning Source LLC
Chambersburg PA
CBHW031333290526
45784CB00014B/2659